Self-Esteem

Implementing A Strategy Of Cultivating Healthy
Emotional Distance To Address Codependency Within
Relationships And Relinquish Tendencies Towards
Excessive Control

Harvey Copeland

TABLE OF CONTENT

Techniques For Developing Self-Confidence......1

The Transformative Impact Of Positive Affirmations On One's Life 10

How To Encourage Introvert Creativity............ 16

Objective Establishment And Progression Towards Goals 49

Togetherness Of The Strategies 57

Can Low Self-Esteem Be Classified As A Mental Health Issue? 66

Changing Loss Into Victory 87

What Factors Contribute To The Erosion Of Our Self-Confidence?.. 127

Techniques For Developing Self-Confidence

The forthcoming discourse will present uncomplicated strategies that can readily be incorporated into one's daily routine, ultimately fostering the cultivation of self-assurance. Do not misconstrue their simplicity. These techniques can yield profound impacts on your overall experience.

The Significance of Internal Dialogues

Prior to commencing our discussion on techniques, it is imperative to address the significance of 'self-talk.' As previously indicated, the articulation of words that emanate from one's speech - including self-perception, perceptions of others, and perceptions of one's circumstances - directly influences the overall quality of life experienced. Should you have not previously encountered this information, do not hold yourself accountable; I myself went a complete 42 years without being privy to this knowledge. It is imperative that you commence to have faith in the information I have just imparted. It is crucial to acknowledge that we exist within a vast energetic realm that is inherently connected to and influenced by vibrational waves. Your speech functions as a transmitter, emitting radiowave-like frequencies that intertwine with compatible streams within this field. The usage of unfavorable words gives rise to a pessimistic existence. Positive vocabulary creates a favorable and uplifting encounter. Both Buddha and Jesus emphasized the profound influence of our words in shaping our reality, emphasizing the importance of exercising caution and wisdom in our choice of language. It is imperative that we do not dismiss this statement without due consideration, as it holds pivotal significance in facilitating transformation.

Flash-Cards

Utilizing flashcards containing pre-determined affirmations pertaining to your personal attributes provides an exceptional method to effectively combat ingrained patterns of negative self-dialogue. By accessing a readily accessible set of flashcards, you can dispel initial disparaging thoughts and redirect your focus towards the uplifting affirmations inscribed upon them, fostering a more positive mindset.

Utilizing flashcards is undeniably the most uncomplicated and effortless approach for implementing change, while ensuring that the efficacy remains intact.

Technique Instructions:

To commence, it is imperative that you allocate a significant amount of time for introspection, contemplating the individual you aspire to transform into or the ideal self-concept you wish to adopt. Proceed by diligently recording all of these reflections. Subsequently, it is recommended to transcribe those thoughts into individual affirmations, following the previously mentioned approach, exemplified by the phrase "I am bold and confident."

In conclusion, ensure that you have the flash-cards readily accessible and retrieve them whenever you identify any instances of engaging in self-deprecating thoughts. Reorient your thought process through the practice of meditation, focusing specifically on the statements provided on your flash-cards. If you articulate them repetitively, audibly, it would be even more advantageous!

Journaling

Now contemplate how you can utilize and exploit that sacred portal and physiological procedure to your advantage. Consider the potential transformation of your thoughts, emotions, and actions through the consistent practice of dedicating time to documenting your reflections on topics of your preference.

Engaging in the practice of journaling confers numerous benefits, making it a transformative activity.

Technique Instructions:

In order to partake in this methodology, it is imperative to comprehend that the style of journaling being referred to is distinct from that of a personal diary or a mere chronicle of daily activities aimed at enhancing one's life and achieving goals. This approach entails establishing a profound bond between oneself and the Divine—an avenue to access the subconscious and tap into the boundless realm of Infinite Intelligence. It is a contemplative methodology that will restructure your neurological patterns, cognitive processes, and belief systems. It is powerful!

In order to commence, it is necessary to possess a journal. I commenced my work by utilizing yellow legal notepads. Ensure that you do not commit the error of becoming entangled and postponing the execution of this procedure merely due to the absence of a "suitable" or aesthetically pleasing journal.

Following that, choose one of your self-affirming "I am" declarations, a scripture passage, or even a cherished quote that imparts wisdom (I have even embarked on Yoda's renowned maxim, "Do. Or do not."). There is no try."). Regardless of your selection, please transcribe it at the beginning of a page in your journal and subsequently peruse it quietly within the confines of your thoughts. Commence the process of documenting all thoughts that arise in your consciousness, refraining from any form of self-censorship. Please refrain from being concerned about grammar or the logical structure of your writing; simply continue writing until you feel a sense of completion.

To fully capitalize on this technique, particularly when handling scriptural texts, it is advisable to meticulously transcribe each keyword as individual entities, subsequently conducting thorough research to ascertain their respective definitions. Occasionally, one may be astounded by the tendency to overlook words and their connotations, and by the frequency with which we misconstrue their intended meanings as a result of unfamiliarity with different cultures and misguided usage. I advise rephrasing the scripture by utilizing the lexical explication, as it aids in dissecting the text from a contemporary perspective. This technique is incredibly impactful and exceedingly thought-provoking to employ.

Nevertheless, upon completion of your journaling, simply proceed to analyze the content you have documented. This step might present a challenge, hence it is advisable not to hasten through it solely for the sake of completion. Remember, you have established a connection with and have recently received guidance from the Divine. Allocate sufficient time for self-reflection and assimilation. This constitutes a crucial aspect of altering your subconscious, your perception of oneself, and ultimately, your life.

The Transformative Impact Of Positive Affirmations On One's Life

Maintaining a positive mental attitude is the key to finding both happiness and accomplishment in life.

Considerations play a pivotal role in shaping our emotions and fostering optimistic thinking.

Positivity fosters an optimistic outlook in individuals, whereas negativity leads to diminished confidence.

It is evident that you have been missing out on a significant abundance in your life. We so frequently work

We often fail to recognize our tendency to negate situations and bypass our own responsibilities, which is a common occurrence.

As we engage in introspection, various considerations permeate our thoughts, leading us to diminish our own abilities to an excessive extent.

and instigate the propagation of uncertainty. There is a limited range of fundamental equipment at your disposal.

Throughout the day, make an effort to replace these negative thoughts and instill a more positive mindset.

Adopting a optimistic viewpoint; incorporating daily affirmations of positivity can enhance the quality of your life.

definitely. They have the capability to instill a growing sense of confidence, heighten mindfulness, bolster self-assurance, and catalyze multi-faceted personal transformation for the better.

What are positive affirmations?

Positive affirmations can be employed throughout the day, regardless of location or time.

If you require their assistance, the greater frequency you employ them, the more readily optimistic thoughts shall supplant negative ones.

By adopting positive practices, you will witness beneficial outcomes manifesting in your life. A statement is a fundamental approach

This approach is employed to transform the often unconscious habit of engaging in negative self-talk into adopting a more positive outlook on one's own life. The

The majority of our population has long been enveloped by pessimistic thoughts, therefore transitioning one's mindset would be beneficial.

The factors to be considered and the thought process will not happen inadvertently but rather, if perchance...

It is imperative that you continue to prioritize obtaining certifications, as they will prove to be effective once you have successfully reoriented your perspective. There

There exists a diverse array of procedures to handle various situations in everyday existence, with the most popular and effective ones enumerated below.

The mirror technique

This practice promotes self-acceptance and cultivates a state of mindfulness and self-assurance.

It is advisable to stand in front of a mirror, preferably a full-length one, while you are either wearing plain attire or underwear.

ter still stripped. Commencing from the top of your head and proceeding through each part of your physique, publicly declare the nature of your being.

You may express appreciation for various parts of your body, such as stating, "I am particularly fond of the way in which my

- The hair glistens, revealing subtle tonal variations where it catches the light. - The eyes possess a stunning radiance.

Nuance of _ _. They possess a radiant and lustrous quality; my vision is captivated by their magnificent presence.

In a methodical manner, progress through your entire exercise regimen while gradually cultivating a more optimistic perception of yourself.

The anywhere technique

This method can be applied anywhere and at any time when you find yourself contemplating a

When you become aware of a negative thought, contemplate relinquishing it

Adjust the volume control within your mind so as to lower it to a level that is not disruptive.

to listen to it any further At that juncture, consider affirming the positive in lieu of the negative and proceed to amplify the intensity, repeating it internally.

The trash can technique

If by any chance you happen to have negative thoughts, it would be advisable to transcribe them onto a piece of paper.

Crush the paper into a compact shape and casually discard it in the waste receptacle, thereby symbolizing the realization that these thoughts hold no value and should be disposed of.

The meditation technique

Find a serene location where you are able to relax and rejuvenate for a brief period of 5 to 10 minutes. Take a moment to close your eyes and unwind.

Allow your rationality to supersede any subjective factors and feelings. Commence the process of reiterating your assertion to your interlocutor.

Continuously reflect upon oneself, concentrating on the verbiage being reiterated and placing faith in the assertions being made.

How To Encourage Introvert Creativity

Introverts possess an innate inclination towards creativity, a fact that has remained largely unrecognized by many. Your aptitude for the systematic arrangement and dissection of factual information bestows upon you greater advantages than you may presently realize. Fundamentally, this is the process by which ingenious notions are conceptualized and brought into existence, thereby affording introverted individuals the most profound advantage.

Considering this information, it is of utmost importance for you to further enhance this inherent ability as it will yield numerous benefits. Many individuals commonly perceive that entrepreneurship is reliant on boldness and willingness to take risks. However, it is crucial to acknowledge that possessing a significant capacity for imagination is equally imperative for achieving prosperity in the business world. The identical illustration applies to education as well. It is widely believed that a high level of intelligence is a prerequisite for success in this field. Unbeknownst to them, it is the practice of accomplished individuals to employ their cognitive faculties for the purpose of innovation rather than mere memorization.

In order to fully unlock the immense capabilities of your introverted mind, it is imperative to establish and engage in routines that foster the nurturing of your inherent creativity. Prior to proceeding, it is essential that you acknowledge and effectively manage any impediments that are obstructing your progress towards attaining this goal.

Overcoming Creativity Killers

Fundamentally, the key impediment to fostering creativity lies within oneself. While you may possess knowledge regarding the mechanisms of your cognition and the areas in which you excel, placing trust in oneself necessitates a distinct and alternative methodology. This book has the potential to consistently affirm the brilliance of your introverted mind, yet without adequate investment of trust and faith in yourself, its significance will be futile.

The following are three predominant states of mind that should be cultivated and controlled in order to unlock and foster your creative potential.

1. Believing that one lacks creativity.

Do not construe this as exclusive to individuals in the artistic realm, such as painters, sculptors, musicians, and the like. Each individual possesses their own unique form of creativity, which can manifest even in the most basic act of verbal expression. Engaging in any form of original action or contemplating ideas necessitates a certain degree of imaginative thinking, and this is a habitual occurrence in your everyday life - whether it pertains to the manner in which you communicate with others or in your attempts to anticipate the outcome of a particular event.

2. Fear of failure.

One may recognize their ingenuity and conceive numerous innovative notions; however, a lack of courage to implement them will result in their squander. Numerous individuals abstained from actualizing their formulated ideas owing to apprehensions about potential failure. It is justifiable to experience a certain level of fear due to its corresponding implications. Nevertheless, this represents the utmost pinnacle of what an individual can anticipate. Failures not only possess extensive teachings, but they also serve as indications of advancement. Consider them as a means of identifying the shortcomings within your plans or methods. Identifying any gaps allows for the opportunity to make further enhancements.

3. Being too judgmental.

An overemphasis on critical thinking can stifle creativity, as it fosters a mindset where ideas are dismissed as unworkable even before exploration.

Please refrain from misconstruing this as an expression of apprehension towards failure. Displaying excessive judgment is akin to doubting the potential for success in a concept, whereas the latter denotes an absence of confidence in one's own capability to succeed.

Eliminating or regulating these obstacles should be your initial step towards enhancing your creativity. The subsequent matter you ought to be aware of pertains to the practices one should embrace.

Cultivating Creativity

Several of the listed attributes are inherently present in individuals with introverted tendencies. Nevertheless, the majority of these actions are executed subconsciously. In order to foster the development of one's creativity, it is necessary to engage in these habits with conscious awareness.

1. Continue to seek knowledge.

Data serves as the principal component of ingenuity. The generation of unique ideas necessitates the existence of preexisting ones, as previously elucidated, whereby these pieces of information are deconstructed and reconstructed in order to attain fresh insights and formulate inventive concepts.

Nonetheless, individuals must exercise discretion when it comes to the acquisition of knowledge. For instance, consider the act of indulging in television viewing all day. Certain individuals may perceive this as a means to acquire knowledge and satisfy their informational needs, to a certain extent. Nevertheless, anticipating the forthcoming developments within the chosen reality television program runs counter to the intended objective.

The most effective means of acquiring new knowledge is through active engagement in the process of studying, which is not necessarily reliant on enrolling in a university. Creativity emerges through the amalgamation of various elements, including factual knowledge, acquired skills, theoretical frameworks, and similar components. Choosing to acquire knowledge in an alternative language or musical instrument can serve as favorable choices.

Please be reminded that the knowledge acquired from this endeavor is not confined solely to its intended purpose. Your introspective mindset will inherently perceive the procedures executed in order to achieve it, and the information it gathers from this is essential. Put simply, the methods serve as the key to enhancing your creativity, such as acquiring the skill of playing a piano. There is no necessity for you to attain proficiency in this matter. The crucial aspect is your comprehension of the mathematical principles it incorporates to generate music. Therefore, this information can be employed in conjunction with other data to generate innovative concepts.

2. Fire up your curiosity.

Continuously pursue knowledge about the 'what'. Persist in inquiring and pursuing solutions to the inquiries of the 'why', 'where', 'when', 'who', and 'how'. Your brain bears resemblance to a receptacle for currency. The quantity you invest corresponds to the quantity you withdraw. Put simply, the range or intricacy of your ideas will principally hinge upon your level of knowledge.

Building upon the illustration presented in the previous narrative, in addition to analyzing the methods employed in acquiring piano proficiency, there exists an abundant array of knowledge that can be sought through this pursuit. Why was the piano invented? How was it conceptualized? From whence and at what time did it have its inception? May I inquire as to the individual responsible for its inception? From what substance are the piano strings composed? By what means did notes and chords attain manifestation? - Additionally, many other items of interest can be found.

It should be noted, nonetheless, that the distinction between this and the top-ranking option lies in its requirement for additional exertion on your part. This will require research. Fortunately, a multitude of answers to your potential inquiries can be readily accessed through the Internet. All that remains for you to accomplish is to craft a query, input it into the search engine of Google, and peruse the resulting entries.

3. The notion of a foolish idea is non-existent.

Surprisingly, there are reputable products in the market that were initially perceived as unintelligent. It is essential to bear in mind that individuals attain legendary status through their triumph over seemingly unachievable feats. An exemplary instance can be found in the iconic Yellow Smiley Face. This widely recognized emblem holds global reverence, and as a result of this seemingly imprudent notion, its architects have now amassed substantial wealth.

In the future, please refrain from dismissing any ideas on the basis of perceived insignificance. Explore and examine the concept thoroughly while fostering its potential, as it holds the possibility to propel you towards accomplishment.

4. Engage in further reading, actively listen to others, broaden your

observations, and increase your consumption of food.

Books, audio-visual creations, artistic visual representations, and indeed, culinary creations, all emanate from the depths of human creativity. Encircling yourself with such elements can evoke a sense of creativity within you.

5. Do not entertain the prospect of adverse reactions from others.

Analogous to the aforementioned observation, concepts are often disregarded due to apprehensions surrounding public opinions. The utmost they can present to you is their viewpoint, and these subjective assessments inherently lack substantial evidence beyond indicating your susceptibility to their impact.

Additionally, it is virtually impossible to forecast the responses of individuals. The aforementioned ideas, when examined through an alternate vantage point, may be regarded as mere fallacies. In order to stimulate the generation of ideas within your mind, it is imperative to exercise restraint and moderation over these thoughts, as they possess the potential to confine and restrict your thinking process.

6. Identify commonalities among two disparate entities and principles.

This is an intellectually stimulating cognitive task, with the assurance of fostering an individual's imaginative aptitude. In this scenario, you would engage in the process of choosing two distinct items, such as a book and a table, for example. Both items are constructed from wood and serve the purpose of containing objects (books are a means of containing knowledge, whereas a table functions to hold miscellaneous items). After recognizing these associations, one proceeds to investigate the potentiality of how tables themselves can convey information, and the manner in which books can be utilized in bolstering alternative objects.

7. Engage yourself with the splendor of the natural world.

The natural environment possesses the capability to evoke cognitive and sensory responses that surpass the potential of artificial mechanisms. It possesses the ability to access our profound essence and inundate us with inspiration, much like how witnessing the sunset from the summit of a mountain, with a serene shoreline below, can invigorate our souls. The capacity of our intellect has a direct impact on our ability to imagine, yet emotions can function as a catalyst when applied to this cognitive process. To put it differently, your creative capabilities will be elevated.

8. Occasionally sign out of your account.

The advent of smartphones enabled individuals to access their email and social media platforms at regular intervals of fifteen minutes. This does not facilitate the cultivation of your creative abilities, as it diverts our attention away from deep thought and reflection. Our minds serve as a fertile ground for nurturing profound ideas, necessitating periods of solitude. The disruption and insistence on prompt response from these platforms divert attention from critical thinking, potentially leading to impulsive and unrefined ideas.

By innate disposition, introverts possess profound creative abilities, and the following recommendations serve as supplementary approaches to amplify this characteristic. It is strongly advised, should you desire to unlock the utmost potential of your mind, to engage in the cultivation of these habits.

3.2 Enhance Your Emotional Coping Skills

Maintaining an optimistic mindset is of utmost significance when it comes to cultivating self-assurance and establishing harmonious relations with the world. Positive thinking entails effectively navigating challenging circumstances, endeavoring to perceive difficult situations from a different perspective, achieving closure in the face of loss, and cultivating resilience to persevere amidst adversity. It is many things. Each individual's perception of positive thinking will be unique. There exist profound and manifold justifications for acquiring the ability to engage in positive thinking. The correlation between our thoughts and our physical well-being is profound. The interaction between the body and the mind is a reciprocal process, wherein the body exerts a profound influence on thoughts and emotions. When individuals establish a pattern of consistently engaging in negative thinking that diminishes their own well-being and that of those around them, it results in unfavorable consequences impacting their overall state. The encounter will lead to a deterioration of various aspects of your well-being, including muscle tension and immune system functioning.

Are you familiar with the saying, "one's dietary intake shapes their identity"? There exists an alternative rendition of that expression which I derive pleasure from, which can be stated as follows: "Your thoughts shape your essence." Engaging in negative self-reflection and harboring pessimistic thoughts about oneself contributes to a self-deprecating mindset and a cycle of self-fulfilling prophecies. By consistently engaging in self-deprecating thoughts that label oneself as indolent and lacking value, an individual inadvertently reinforces and perpetuates behavior patterns deemed worthless or idle. One begins to contemplate oneself as the most unfavorable manifestation of one's own idenitity. This is an issue that must be combated. Maintaining an optimistic mindset significantly enhances one's holistic well-being. Positive thinking has the potential to enhance not only one's mood and attention span, but also their physical well-being.

If you are experiencing symptoms indicative of an emotional disorder that significantly impede your daily functioning, it would be advantageous for you to undergo a mental health evaluation conducted by a qualified medical practitioner or other esteemed professionals in the field. Depression is a prevalent phenomenon within our society, attributed to a disturbance or dysregulation of one's emotional state. Depression constitutes a compilation of symptoms. These comprise a range of symptoms such as diminished motivation, disturbances in sleep patterns, excessive sleep, inadequate or excessive eating patterns, social withdrawal, and other potential manifestations. A considerable factor lies in the absence of sufficient drive or determination. It engenders individuals to become trapped within a perpetual cycle. They experience a lack of self-esteem and motivation, resulting in their lack of action, which subsequently leads to feelings of self-doubt and regret. The cycle perpetuates ad infinitum. Treating this condition can be challenging due to the inherent difficulty in recognizing depression-induced lack of motivation. It is merely an influence that has assumed control over your state of awareness. The absence of drive to improve is a contributing factor in the issue. What methods can be employed to cultivate motivation within an individual? There is a prevailing concept that posits the idea that action precedes motivation. This concept is intriguing as it embraces an unconventional approach by propelling what seems to be regressive to the forefront. One might assume that motivation comes before action; one first deliberates on the reasons behind wanting to undertake a particular task, and subsequently proceeds to take the necessary steps to accomplish it. This concept posits that motivation is a result of preceding action. This signifies that it is necessary to take action even in the absence of motivation.

If one is able to convey this understanding to an individual, it could potentially influence their cognitive perspective. The point you are endeavoring to communicate is not that motivation comes after taking action, but rather that taking action leads to motivation. It may be a concise expression, yet it holds significant meaning. That statement has the ability to penetrate the fog of indifference that can be generated by the presence of depression.

Factors contributing to reduced self-confidence

Individuals afflicted with low self-esteem frequently experience a pervasive sense of self-deprecation and harbor feelings of inferiority in comparison to others. Consequently, these individuals face an elevated risk of being unable to realize their full capabilities. Considering their lack of proactive behavior in establishing and striving towards their objectives, there is a risk of insufficient dedication towards crucial matters such as their education and professional endeavors. They tend to exhibit a greater susceptibility towards accepting mistreatment from individuals in their social circles, including friends, family members, and romantic partners. Studies have indicated a correlation between low self-esteem in teenagers

and adolescents and the manifestation of these detrimental behaviors.
- Unlawful Conduct ● Illicit Actions ● Deviant Behavior ● Misdeeds ● Unlawful Activities
- Adolescent pregnancy ● Pregnancy among teenagers ● Pregnancy during adolescence
- Withdrawing from an educational institution ● Discontinuing one's education ● Terminating enrollment in a school
- Substandard scholastic achievement ● Inadequate educational outcomes ● Lack of satisfactory academic progress ● Unsatisfactory scholastic attainment
- Substance misuse and substance dependency
- Eating disorders
- Premature initiation of sexual behavior

The phenomenon of experiencing low self-esteem encompasses intricacies beyond a mere negative emotional state. Insufficient self-confidence can have a significant impact on individuals' wellbeing. Despite the challenges involved in quantifying the prevalence of low self-esteem, numerous scientific investigations have yielded compelling findings indicating a notable decline in self-esteem among individuals as they approach adolescence. Individuals within this particular demographic frequently develop a belief that they fall short in various domains, including but not limited to interpersonal relationships, physical attractiveness, and scholastic achievements.

When individuals experience the onset of low self-esteem during their formative years, there is an increased likelihood that it will persist into adulthood. At this juncture, it commences to impede crucial matters such as an individual's capacity to lead a gratifying and well-being-oriented existence. An essential element of self-esteem is its subjective nature, rendering it inherently disconnected from objective reality and resistant to permanence. The root of self-esteem can occasionally be discerned, however, the notion that one's perceptions of oneself are immutable is an erroneous belief.

Self-esteem is a cognitive pattern that remains malleable and subject to transformation. An individual possessing robust self-esteem has the capacity to transition into a state of diminished self-esteem, but conversely, they also possess the potential to reverse this trajectory. One can only effectively enhance their self-esteem if they demonstrate a willingness to recognize and confront the adverse evaluations they hold about themselves. Irrespective of the degree of conviction an individual possesses regarding their present self-assessment, there are considerable benefits to be gained and no disadvantages to be incurred by embracing the notion that they possess the ability to govern their own self-esteem. By deliberately opting to question their own cognitive processes, individuals can initiate a transformation in their thought patterns and subsequent decision-making in both the present and future. Listed below are several prevalent factors contributing to individuals experiencing low self-esteem. This enumeration might aid in the recognition of potential influences in your life that might be contributing to your diminished self-esteem.

Parents who lack involvement or exhibit negligence in their child's upbringing.

Virtually all individuals, particularly during their early years, experience profound introspection influenced by the manner in which they are treated by those closest to them during this period. This statement holds particularly strong when referring to the parents or guardians of these individuals. Undoubtedly, it is universally acknowledged that every individual is entitled to nurturing familial connections; however, regrettably, certain individuals have been deprived of the affection and assistance that are fundamentally essential for all. In such instances, the parents frequently experience mental health challenges or similar concerns which render them incapable of adequately tending to their children's needs and providing them with the requisite attention and guidance they both require and deserve. This gives rise to significant self-esteem issues among individuals at a tender age, as their caregivers fail to fulfill their responsibilities adequately.

Negative Peers

In a parallel manner to the impact that parents/guardians have on individuals with low self-esteem, the influence of peers during their formative years is equally significant. If an individual belongs to a social cohort wherein they consistently face disrespect, discouragement, disregard for their perspectives and emotions, or coercion into activities that elicit discomfort, it can result in them perceiving personal inadequacy. This notion fosters the belief that one can only gain acceptance from others by conforming to their desires and abandoning one's own perspectives and viewpoints. This has the potential to cause significant harm to an individual's self-image and confidence.

Trauma

When an individual undergoes instances of physical, emotional, or sexual abuse, it frequently elicits sentiments of shame and guilt within said individual. The individual might hold a mistaken belief that they have committed actions justifying the mistreatment, or that they are undeserving of the affection, regard, and consideration of the person inflicting the abuse. Individuals who have been subjected to abuse may experience a multitude of anxiety and depression symptoms, which hinder their capacity to lead a joyous and gratifying existence.

Body Image

According to recent scientific studies, it has been observed that nearly half of adolescent females express dissatisfaction with their body image, with this proportion increasing significantly to almost 80% by the time they reach the age of 17. In a comparable investigation, it was discovered that a considerable proportion of adolescent boys (30%) and adolescent girls (50%) frequently engaged in detrimental practices with the intent of altering their weight to attain their desired physique.

These behaviors encompassed smoking tobacco, abstaining from meals, inducing vomiting, employing laxatives, and engaging in fasting.

Body image holds great importance, particularly in females, when it comes to the self-esteem of young individuals. Since the inception of womanhood, females have been exposed to unattainable portrayals of the ideal female physique, fostering a culture wherein certain body types are regarded as the epitome of attractiveness. This media-driven objectification has relegated women's bodies to little more than visual commodities, perpetuating the notion that their physicality solely exists for the consumption, scrutiny, and exploitation of others. As the onset of puberty occurs and prompts natural changes in a girl's body, the absence of media portrayals depicting these changes often results in feelings of powerlessness and diminished self-perception in terms of attractiveness.

Adolescent males also encounter challenges regarding negative body perception. Numerous individuals encounter similar challenges, reminiscent of women, such as issues concerning weight and body composition. Nevertheless, the youth tend to prioritize their muscle mass. In contrast to women, it is important to note that the male physique is not regarded as an object for the consumption of others; rather, it holds symbolic significance as a representation of masculinity. Adolescent males frequently experience societal expectations for attaining muscular physiques as a means to showcase their physical prowess and masculinity, consequently leading to insecurities regarding their stature, a characteristic beyond their control.

Insignificantly Sized Fish in a Vast Aquatic Habitat

Young individuals may easily perceive themselves as engulfed by the vastness of the world. This sensation engenders sentiments of insignificance, impotence, and inefficacy. A lot of young people don't feel these feelings until they head into adulthood, but it is still possible that younger people experience through the famous "existential crisis." This is where a person goes through the thoughts of questioning life itself. Inquiries pertaining to one's existential purpose such as "What is the meaning of my existence?" Queries about the essence of existence and one's pursuit of meaning hold significant pertinence, and the absence of satisfactory answers presents a substantial peril to an individual's perception of their own value.

Unrealistic Goals

When individuals encounter internal or external pressures, emanating from sources such as figures of authority or their social circle, certain individuals may develop overly high expectations in regard to their accomplishments, encompassing aspects like societal standing and involvement in extracurricular activities. Individuals who may be facing academic challenges may hold the belief that they must consistently obtain perfect grades, whereas those who excel academically may inadvertently assume numerous additional responsibilities and anticipate the same level of success in all of them. Individuals who actively pursue popularity may prioritize garnering universal approval and may experience apprehension regarding potential disapproval from others, despite the fact that achieving universal popularity is unattainable for any individual, regardless of their status. It is utterly impossible to satisfy all individuals. The inherent probability of experiencing failure when pursuing these impractical objectives contributes to individuals' perception of personal inadequacy.

Previous Bad Choices

Frequently, individuals find themselves entangled in a repetitive cycle of decision-making and action that is perpetuated by habitual behavior. This could stem from factors such as this individual's lack of attentiveness in academic settings, previous shortcomings as a friend, or involvement in risky activities, including drug use and hazardous behaviors. They might develop the perception that they are inherently predisposed to behaving in such manners. Frequently, individuals can develop a negative perception of themselves as a result of their previous poor choices, and they harbor a sense of skepticism about their present capacity to effect personal change. Consequently, they abstain from making any efforts in this regard. As a consequence, they persist in making decisions that perpetuate their unfavorable self-perception.

Negative Thought Patterns

Once individuals become accustomed to their self-perception and manner of self-expression, this behavior ingrains itself as a tenacious routine difficult to alter. In a manner akin to the concept of muscle memory, when an individual engages in a physical endeavor such as bicycling, the neurological processes within their brain instinctively transmit the necessary instructions to the corresponding muscle groups in order to carry out the requisite actions. The cognitive process of individuals operates in an identical manner. If individuals frequently experience feelings of inferiority or worthlessness, it is probable that they will persistently harbor negative thoughts about themselves, consequently fostering a tendency to perpetuate such thinking patterns unless they are able to initiate a process of actively confronting and challenging those thoughts. Similar to the way in which muscle memory can acquire an incorrect methodology for performing a physical task, our emotions and cognitive processes can likewise acquire erroneous patterns.

The aforementioned factors contributing to low self-esteem are not exhaustive, but rather represent the prevailing causes commonly reported. Cause #8 that has been discovered pertains to negative thought patterns, which tend to be the main instigators behind the enduring presence of low self-esteem in individuals, while disregarding the underlying factors that initially triggered such patterns. Individuals who harbor suspicions regarding their low self-esteem must conduct a thorough examination of their circumstances within the realms of their domestic environment, social interactions, professional endeavors, and educational pursuits. This comprehensive analysis aims to potentially ascertain the origins underlying their diminished self-regard.

Objective Establishment And Progression Towards Goals

Goal setting and striving for goals is an additional domain that warrants utmost caution in our lives, ensuring we do not adopt the perspective of the external world observing us. The prevailing attention of the global observers is predominantly directed towards a specific outcome. It is imperative that our agenda be centered not solely on the outcome, but also on the entire process.

Language plays a significant role in our existence: we utilize it to express ourselves, experience various emotions, strive to embody its essence, and witness its potential to inspire or inflict pain, occasionally evoking a sense of bliss. Moreover, they significantly contribute to making life thoroughly enjoyable.

It is essential for all individuals to understand that attaining any degree of achievement in life can only be achievable if objectives are appropriately established and strategies are clearly defined. This is because achieving clarity of purpose necessitates the establishment of a clearly defined goal and the formulation of a corresponding plan.

Once you have diligently conveyed these two elements, you will possess a distinct comprehension that will function as your compass, given your apparent grasp upon your ultimate objectives.

Establishing objectives and developing a strategic framework would foster a distinct mental visualization and concurrently cultivate a subconscious imprint of that planned vision. By doing so, you are simultaneously providing your subconscious mind with the proper guidance regarding the direction you should pursue when it comes to executing your plan.

This would additionally provide you with the appropriate perspective on how to respond in a suitable manner in the event of any unforeseen circumstances arising throughout the process; undertaking this approach will ensure that your concentration remains steadfast even in the presence of unexpected occurrences.

Maintaining focused and adhering to the goals that you have established is a crucial aspect to bear in mind if you aspire to attain success in any endeavor throughout your life. Concentration is a vital component of goal setting and strategic planning. This is due to the fact that deviating from your primary objective greatly increases the likelihood of losing sight of all the components within your plan, ultimately resulting in its disintegration.

This phenomenon arises due to the confusion that occurs within your subconscious mind, leading it to believe that your original intent or enthusiasm towards the goal has diminished. Simultaneously, you would acquire a state of detachment and apathy towards the objective that you were previously excessively eager to achieve.

It is not quite facile or straightforward to maintain a steadfast concentration on a particular matter. Indeed, maintaining a concentrated focus on a solitary subject appears to present a considerable level of complexity. Why? This is because your mind appears to possess a distinct identity; akin to a completely disengaged and unrelated component from your primary framework.

Attempt to perceive it as a resolute adolescent who refuses to conform to your intended course of action, but instead focuses its efforts on pursuing something contrary to your preferences. This is where the process of goal setting and planning can become intricate.

The essential factor in achieving success in goal setting and planning lies in undertaking actions that capture the focus of your mind and enable it to adapt to changes. This objective can be achieved through maintaining unwavering dedication towards your goals.

You must ensure that unforeseen circumstances should not lead you astray from the initial objective, but rather, influence it to accommodate changes and effectively utilize them to your benefit rather than as obstacles.

When this behavior is consistently and thoroughly practiced, your mind will gradually develop an adaptive capacity to effectively respond to diverse circumstances in an optimistic manner. This will lead you towards the pursuit of actualizing your objectives. This is the reason why maintaining a steadfast dedication to your established objectives is regarded as the fundamental factor that will guide you towards achievements.

The absence of a life purpose is tantamount to lacking direction on our journey through life. For certain individuals, this may appear to be a bold and daring endeavor. However, in the event of an extreme circumstance, it is possible that we may find ourselves in an irreparable situation, leaving us with no choice but to confront and accept the outcomes we encounter for the remainder of our lives.

A significant number of individuals are disinclined to find themselves in such circumstances during the course of their lives. Regrettably, a considerable number of individuals perceive no viable solution to their current undesirable circumstances and consequently endure lifelong suffering. Nevertheless, they are unaware of the fact that they have the potential to transcend their suffering and embrace a life characterized by prosperity and joy.

Consider envisioning yourself formulating a strategic itinerary for a forthcoming excursion to a sun-soaked coastal destination, meticulously preparing an assortment of provisions, ensuring that the journey exudes not just comfort, but also holds the potential to create cherished memories.

Your entire family or accompanied friends would surely be filled with excitement and eagerly anticipate the merriment that awaits them during the entire beach excursion. It is possible that you may observe time passing swiftly, where hours resemble minutes and minutes resemble seconds.

By way of comparison, consider a scenario where you and your companions embark on a spontaneous journey without any prior deliberation regarding your destination. Similar to an unsettling dream transformed into reality, one may ultimately find themselves in a state of aimlessness, having veered off course and becoming trapped within an environment devoid of possibilities for action. Your acquaintances express their dissatisfaction with your decision to embark on this dreadful excursion. One may experience a profound sense of powerlessness and embarrassment.

It is essential for individuals to engage in strategic planning and establish concrete objectives in both the short-term and long-term in order to attain success.

Envision the desired destination you aspire to achieve in a span of five years, and proceed to deconstruct your overarching five-year strategy into increments of one-year short-term plans. Having shorter plans helps you in monitoring your progress and take necessary and appropriate corrective measures along the way.

Togetherness Of The Strategies

It is our comprehension that at some point in time, you began to harbor dissatisfaction towards your own existential being. The origins of this occurrence remain uncertain, as it is unclear whether it emerged from criticism, rebuff, or the influences exerted by parents or peers. What can be ascertained is that the impact of this particular sentiment is alike, as it serves to constrain one's self-confidence. To put it differently, it seems that you harbor uncertainties regarding your own abilities, consequently leading to a deficiency in self-assurance.

We provided you with an extensive discussion on different strategies, and upon initial examination, this is the recommended course of action for overcoming your present lack of confidence:

Familiarize yourself with your negative triggers – Put simply, gain a comprehensive understanding of the origins of this negativity. This empowers you to effectively disregard the negative aspects and concentrate on leveraging positive factors to counterbalance them. The greater extent of disapproval or negative feedback you have received, the more imperative it becomes to focus on cultivating self-acceptance. The opinions of others hold no significance in regard to your being. They are not obligated to live the life that you do. You do. It is imperative that you acknowledge and distance yourself from detrimental influences. Once you identify the catalysts or factors that evoke negative emotions within you, you can proactively take measures to restrict your interactions with them. Should this occurrence be confined to your cognitive processes, we have likewise elucidated the utilization of mindfulness as a means to disengage from said ruminations.

Negative stimuli can arise from contemplation on individuals who have betrayed one or apprehension towards being in the presence of individuals who elicit a sense of unease and dissatisfaction with oneself. Consider carefully the individuals within your social circle and assess which acquaintances bring about a sense of well-being and positivity in your presence, while also identifying those individuals that elicit feelings of unease and self-doubt. What situations trigger insecurity? It is imperative that you acknowledge them, as until this is done, you will be unable to rectify the situation or prevent potential catalysts. You should establish a means of circumventing the factors that exacerbate your descent into pessimism until such time as you cultivate your level of self-confidence.

Engaging in self-care and cultivating self-worth – The subsequent approach focused on how one nurtures their well-being, urging individuals to approach themselves with kindness and allocate a portion of their time to meaningful endeavors like volunteering. These endeavors play a vital role in enhancing one's self-assurance and fostering a sense of personal fulfillment. These matters did not seek validation from external agents. These initiatives were designed with the objective of enhancing your well-being and promoting self-affirming perspectives on your personal identity. This is so important. You possess equal worth to any individual on Earth, however, persisting in undermining your true potential serves to diminish your levels of self-assurance.

Embracing your life - The approach that encompasses self-affection focuses on cultivating one's individuality and finding gratification in one's preferred pursuits. It is of utmost importance that you engage in such activities, and upon discovering pastimes that truly captivate your interest, you might even encounter individuals who share comparable preferences. Nevertheless, should you relegate these aspirations to a secondary position, you shall perpetually remain unaware of your true aptitude in the endeavors that bring you joy. If you are aware of your availability, utilize it for engaging in constructive pursuits that bring you personal satisfaction. It is incumbent upon oneself to enhance the quality of their life, such that upon awakening each morning, they experience a profound sense of self-fulfillment. In the event that you are unable to accomplish this, there are no alternative individuals capable of achieving it on your behalf.

Respiration and Mindfulness - By integrating this form of practice into your daily routine, it engenders a profound sense of connectivity and aids in harmonizing your perception of self and environment. It is recommended that you make a daily attempt at this. Even allocating a mere half hour a day towards practicing mindfulness can substantially contribute to the development of confidence. Additionally, it is possible to engage in physical activities throughout the day when experiencing profound negativity or apprehension towards engaging in unfamiliar tasks. For instance, by engaging in the practice of mindful breathing prior to a meeting, one can effectively attain a state of mental tranquility, resulting in enhanced cognitive acuity and a greater capacity to actively contribute during the meeting. That's important.

Starting from the instant you arise in the morning until the point in time you retire for the night, it is imperative that these strategies become an integral component of your daily existence. Know who you are. Embrace your true self and refrain from imposing upon yourself the expectations established by others. Alternatively, failing to do so may result in insufficiency, giving rise to the occurrence of diminished self-assurance.

One can employ the practice of mindfulness to eliminate detrimental thought patterns. Rather than succumbing to negative thoughts like "I am incapable of completing this task," it would be advisable to shift your mindset towards the present moment and observe your surroundings. Embrace the weather with enthusiasm. Embrace the opportunity bestowed upon you with enthusiasm and take deep breaths, allowing serenity to reignite your determination for a fresh attempt. Indeed, there will exist certain limitations to what one can achieve in life. However, on occasion, it becomes imperative to persevere diligently and derive gratification from the realization that one possesses a greater degree of adaptability than originally presumed. Avoid convincing yourself of your own limitations. Remind yourself that every instance in your life presents a fresh occasion to engage in new experiences and discern their suitability for integration into your life.

Can Low Self-Esteem Be Classified As A Mental Health Issue?

Although low self-esteem does not constitute a standalone psychological well-being issue, it is undeniably intertwined with it. If a multitude of factors exert a prolonged impact on one's self-esteem, it can potentially engender mental health complications such as depression or anxiety.

Self-esteem, in its utmost breadth, pertains to the extent to which an individual attributes value to their own personhood. Self-esteem is intertwined with an individual's ability to maintain a positive mindset towards oneself and uphold such constructive beliefs, particularly in challenging circumstances, especially those involving evaluation by others.

Adults with elevated levels of global self-esteem are likely to experience increased levels of prosperity, improved social interactions, and enhanced job satisfaction compared to their counterparts. Low self-esteem is correlated with various issues, such as mental health disorders, substance abuse, and eating disorders. Although self-esteem is generally considered to be a stable aspect of one's personality, it also fluctuates based on recent failures or successes. Additionally, there are subcategories of self-esteem that pertain to specific domains of an individual's life, such as sports and leisure activities.

Perhaps due to its unique characteristics, the concept of self-esteem has been extensively explored in psychological literature. However, notwithstanding its disjointed definition, the notion of self-esteem has been extensively scrutinized, particularly through empirical investigations conducted within communities. It has been extensively researched in relation to emotional well-being and the overall quality of life, across various domains including educational institutions, professional environments, and recreational activities.

Self-Concept and Self-Esteem

The perceptions and evaluations that individuals have of themselves determine their sense of identity, their capabilities, and their potential for growth and transformation. These remarkable internal influences provide individuals with an innate regulatory mechanism, effectively directing and upholding their behavior, whilst guiding them throughout their journey in life. The self-concept and self-esteem are frequently referred to as individuals' perceptions and feelings regarding themselves. These attributes, coupled with their ability to navigate the challenges of life and exert influence over their circumstances.

Self-concept is defined as the collective compilation of an individual's beliefs and knowledge regarding their own personal associates and attributes. It is categorized as a subjective concept that categorizes theoretical and substantial aspects regarding oneself and regulates the processing of self-relevant information.

Alternative phrasing in a formal tone: Various conceptualizations, such as self-perception and self-reflection, serve as corollaries to the concept of self. Self-esteem can be defined as the objective assessment and pragmatic assessment of one's self-image, and is considered synonymous with self-regard, self-valuation, and self-value. It refers to the comprehensive evaluation of one's positive or negative value, denoting the self-assigned ratings an individual assigns to themselves across various aspects and domains of life.

Self-worth as a mitigating element

Self-esteem is not only regarded as a foundational aspect of psychological well-being, but it also serves as a safeguard that contributes to enhanced well-being and positive social behavior by functioning as a buffer against the influence of adverse effects. It is observed to significantly promote a stable and prosperous work environment, evident in aspects of life such as accomplishments, success, contentment, and resilience in the face of diseases like cancer and heart ailments.

Conversely, an unstable self-perception and diminished self-worth can play a pivotal role in the manifestation of various psychological and social ailments, such as depression, anorexia nervosa, bulimia, anxiety, aggression, substance abuse, and reckless behaviors. These circumstances not solely lead to a significant degree of personal anguish but also impose a substantial burden on society. As demonstrated, upcoming assessments have indicated low self-esteem as a risk factor and positive self-esteem as a mitigating factor.

In summary, self-esteem is regarded as a compelling factor in both physical and emotional well-being. As a result, it should be a significant focal point in the promotion of overall wellness, particularly in the context of mental health. Well-being promotion refers to the process of empowering individuals to exert control over and enhance their personal well-being. The management of emotions, together with overall wellness, is widely regarded as a fundamental aspect of the concept of well-being.

Self-perception and self-worth are integral elements of emotional welfare, thereby serving as crucial pillars of psychological well-being.

According to Furnham and Cheng (2000), self-esteem has been found to be the predominant and remarkable predictor of happiness. Low self-esteem is a catalyst for personal disorder, whereas positive self-esteem, key principles, and objectives seem to significantly contribute to 'prosperity.' Elements such as self-concept, personality, and confidence represent crucial constituents of emotional well-being.

The manifestation of the resistance factor of self-esteem becomes more apparent in research that examines the impact of stress and physical ailments, where self-esteem functions as a protective barrier against fear and susceptibility. This is evidenced by the perceptions surrounding individuals who are consistently unwell. It has been brought to light that a heightened sense of authority, viability, and strong self-esteem, as well as the presence of a confederate and numerous intimate connections, all directly contribute to a mitigating effect on the progression of depressive symptoms in individuals afflicted with chronic illness. Self-confidence has also been shown to enhance an individual's ability to cope with illness and postoperative recovery.

Enhancing Cognitive Transparency: Steps to Take and Destinations to Pursue?

I was seated, endeavoring to elucidate my aspiration to solely engage in writing and foster my growth as an author. As I progressed, my coach posed increasingly thought-provoking inquiries. Subsequently, a sudden influx of ideas pertaining to my capabilities emerged in my thoughts. Unbeknownst to me, two areas that had escaped my attention were public speaking and professional coaching.

I initiated the creation of a YouTube channel, commenced the production of a podcast, pursued a coaching academy certification, became a member of Toastmasters, and subsequently experienced an abundance of joy.

During my discussions with my coach, I encountered certain challenging inquiries and considerations; nonetheless, I persistently discovered viable pathways to pursue my passion.

The preceding example illustrates the skill of coaching and effectively posing appropriate inquiries. Therefore, I have embarked on a journey to provide coaching assistance, in order to facilitate the experience of similar emotional states in others. When we become cognizant of the myriad possibilities that lie before us, it instills within us a profound sense of exhilaration. The recognition of our inherent potential is synonymous with the recognition of our own personal worth. Hence, engaging in activities such as coaching can significantly contribute to our personal growth and facilitate the realization of a more satisfying and rewarding self.

What distinguishes a coach, mentor, and counsellor from one another?

I've summarised below:

A coach refers to a person who possesses the ability to broaden one's consciousness, assist in the recognition of genuine desires, and facilitate the discovery of suitable alternatives and actions to achieve them.

A mentor refers to an individual who possesses expertise in the desired field and provides explicit guidance on actions that can be taken.

A counselor is an individual who delves into one's past and underlying causes of emotions, aiming to enhance self-awareness. The counsellor or therapist will provide assistance in facilitating the discovery of solutions, rather than actively proposing them.

Action:

It is straightforward on this occasion - enlist the services of a coach, mentor, or counselor. There is a wide array of information available for retrieval on the internet. It represents a commendable investment and does not require a substantial financial outlay.

Engaging in discussions concerning matters of concern is a pivotal advantage.

I entered the premises of my workplace with a more subdued demeanor than my customary level of enthusiasm. I deviated from my customary demeanor.

There existed curiosity among individuals regarding the reason behind the stark contrast in behavior exhibited by an individual who is typically characterized by an extroverted and confident demeanor today. I did not engage in verbal discourse, not even once.

During the period of my parents' phone conversation, I exhibited a more reserved disposition and refrained from engaging in my usual sociable and extroverted behavior. Subsequently, my mother sent me a message to inquire about my well-being and check on my overall state, considering my sudden silence. Once more, I refrained from speaking.

During a phone conversation, my supervisor inquired about my well-being, as several individuals had observed a change in my demeanor and noticed that I was not displaying my usual disposition. I did not talk.

These and numerous other occurrences in my life precipitated feelings of despondency, solitariness, and estrangement. Despite having numerous individuals in my vicinity, I was inadvertently causing harm to myself by suppressing my inner turmoil. On certain occasions, I engaged in brief conversations with others that momentarily improved my state of mind. However, subsequently, I would revert back to feeling profoundly negative about myself and internalize those emotions once more.

I came to the realization that it was necessary for me to adopt a more candid approach when it comes to acknowledging my own emotions and communicating with others. I am willing to make any necessary efforts to enhance my self-esteem, and such action is imperative within this particular realm. I am determined to significantly elevate my self-esteem, which entails increasing my level of communication.

There have been numerous occurrences where I have observed individuals undergo a change in their demeanor and choose not to divulge the reasons behind their transformation. There is a limitation to the extent of influence one can exert in motivating others to engage in conversation, while retaining the ultimate authority to decide whether one engages in conversation with someone else or not. I have discovered that discussing hardships has greatly enhanced my well-being.

I have encountered this statement on numerous occasions and hold the belief that it holds true: 'The act of repressing one's emotions can lead to a state of depression.'

Indeed, I maintain that it is highly self-centered to refrain from engaging in conversation with an individual during times of personal hardship. Let me explain...

When individuals choose to suppress and immobilize their negative emotions, a common sentiment I have come across is, 'I am reticent to impose my unfavorable ruminations upon others'.

There exist individuals who possess a genuine desire to offer assistance, be it acquaintances, relatives, or community networks.

The action of suppressing negative thoughts, such as I was previously engaged in, can be characterized as:

- Cultivating a pessimistic atmosphere that has the potential to adversely affect others (self-centered)

- Elicit concern from others (egocentric)

- Inhibiting the manifestation of one's complete state of happiness to the external world (self-centered)

- Failing to recount one's personal narrative or adversity, thereby neglecting the opportunity to inspire others and alleviate their sense of isolation (self-centered).

Therefore, this statement is not intended as a critique of individuals who frequently suppress their emotions or directed towards my former self. Rather, it serves as an acknowledgment that consistently enduring personal hardships in isolation detrimentally impacts both oneself and those in their vicinity. While it is true that the advantages of opening up extend beyond your personal gains.

Therefore, may we inquire for assistance?

This misconception may arise from our perception that expressing our feelings is an act of self-centeredness, when in reality, suppressing them can be even more self-centered. Additionally, this can be attributed to the apprehension surrounding societal perception and the inherent sense of self-importance one possesses. The ego constitutes a cerebral component responsible for the scrutiny of one's identity or outward perception.

We are concerned that soliciting assistance might result in potential damage to this item.

So, what is the appropriate manner in which we may solicit assistance?

On certain occasions, I pondered whether seeking assistance was an overwhelming endeavor, yet akin to most situations, one must indeed take proactive measures lest nothing be altered.

The initial action of scheduling an appointment with a therapist constituted the primary stage, followed by the subsequent step of documenting the topics I intended to address, culminating in the act of verbal communication during the session.

When engaging in conversation with individuals, we make use of the strengths they possess. The adage "One plus one equals more than two" is indeed accurate. Progress commences with the recognition of truth and the acknowledgment of one's need for assistance. It is a common truth that assistance is often required by individuals in various forms. Therefore, it is advisable to refrain from dismissing the possibility of seeking help by hastily declaring, "I don't need assistance!" Moreover, it is imperative that one steers clear of descending into a state of self-deprecation any further. Seek the guidance of an individual by venturing outside and engaging in conversation, particularly when you find yourself confronted with a sense of confinement or adversity.

Action:

Please document any current concerns or distressing matters that are occupying your thoughts.

Subsequently, enumerate individuals whom you can rely on to engage in a meaningful discussion.

Subsequently, proactively engage in conversation with that individual/those individuals.

There is no alternative method for improving one's conversational skills than engaging in direct oral communication with individuals. It may appear self-evident, yet it consistently serves as a practical admonition.

Changing Loss Into Victory

The majority of individuals have a limited capacity to endure significant letdowns, which eventually diminishes their zeal and redirects their attention towards their diminished self-worth. Learn to direct your attention towards achieving modest accomplishments. Transform those instances of failure into minor triumphs and those minor triumphs into more significant ones.

In the event of initial failure...

The concepts of success and self-esteem are intertwined in a profoundly reciprocal manner. Immediate self-esteem enhancement is a direct result of achieving success. Self-esteem breeds success. They solemnized their matrimony, and together they traverse the journey of life, united in an inseparable bond. Is the age-old saying, "if at first you don't succeed, try, try again," universally recognized as a truism or the most valuable guidance one can receive for enhancing self-esteem?

For individuals who possess low self-esteem, envisioning personal success can prove to be an arduous undertaking. It poses a daunting task for individuals with diminished self-worth to identify and acknowledge accomplishments when they encounter them; particularly, when they come their way.

For certain individuals, achieving success merely equates to enduring and navigating through the challenges of each passing day. For individuals, the journey may involve a genuine transformation from experiencing diminished self-worth to embracing self-validation. This transition necessitates a thorough examination of the events that transpire in one's life, and subsequently implementing necessary alterations. If you persist in maintaining the status quo without making any alterations, it follows that your self-esteem will suffer rather than improve.

Nevertheless, should you examine your conduct, observe your words, and reflect upon your thoughts, implementing even minor alterations shall invariably enhance your self-esteem. As emphasized in the preceding chapter, one's self-esteem can be profoundly influenced by their thoughts, verbal expressions, and internal dialogue. Everything has the potential to materialize in the physical realm - one's thoughts shape one's identity.

When encountering failure, it is crucial to engage in introspection, not merely perceive oneself as a failure, but rather, truly acknowledge the occurrence of failure. Consequently, one should scrutinize the reasons behind such failures and subsequently undertake personal modifications, be they substantial or minor, as a direct consequence of these experiences. Do not fixate on the failure itself; instead, endeavor to understand its underlying causes and enact appropriate modifications. When this action is undertaken, failure transforms into a pathway leading to success.

The experience of failure often serves as a pathway towards achieving success. You will experience an increase in strength rather than a decrease. Instead of experiencing a loss of self-esteem due to failure, you will enhance and elevate your self-confidence. We encounter failures as a means to thoroughly scrutinize the reasons behind them, implement modifications, and subsequently, make renewed attempts. Iterating persistently without implementing any modifications while anticipating a divergent outcome does not align with the definition of achievement. Instead, it is referred to as insane. Nevertheless, in the event of failure, it is imperative to thoroughly evaluate the circumstances, implement necessary adjustments, and persistently strive towards achieving incremental triumphs, leading ultimately to a complete and remarkable accomplishment, thereby enhancing one's self-assurance.

The 'Ah Ha' Moment

An immensely thrilling aspect to anticipate while striving for an increase in self-esteem is the epiphany known as the 'Eureka' moment. What precisely does the term 'Ah Ha' moment denote? It is characterized as an instance of instantaneous or unforeseen revelation or momentous realization. It may entail a critical juncture wherein all aspects become lucid and aligned. The moment of realization, commonly referred to as the 'Ah Ha' moment, possesses the potential to bestow upon individuals an invaluable sense of clarity, subsequently elevating their self-worth.

The phenomenon commonly referred to as the 'Ah Ha' moment is alternatively recognized within certain circles as the eureka effect. This phenomenon manifests throughout the breadth of human experience, wherein a previously unintelligible concept swiftly and immediately becomes comprehensible to one's perception. This particular moment is the one that imparts discernment to you. A comprehensive understanding of reality has the potential to transcend one's self-doubt and low self-esteem, leading to a state of confidence and inner fortitude.

The 'Ah Ha' moment signifies an instance of significant advancement. It is a location wherein individuals can overcome their diminished self-confidence and personal insecurities. Frequently, individuals encounter significant challenges when attempting to overcome the psychological barriers associated with diminished self-worth. The occurrence of an epiphany is exceedingly swift, profoundly illuminating, and unquestionably accurate, as it effortlessly surmounts any barriers and transports you to a realm that lies beyond your familiar confines and surpasses your own perception of your capabilities. Allowing it to happen will result in an augmentation of self-esteem.

Summary and Action Plan

In the present chapter, we embark upon a trajectory that leads to significantly enhanced self-esteem, along with the implementation of mechanisms designed to facilitate the augmentation of one's sense of self-worth. In this fourth step, we present a set of targeted exercises designed to enhance one's self-esteem.

You are your own self. You possess unique qualities, thus it is imperative that you refrain from drawing comparisons between yourself and others. Please compile a inventory enumerating your endowments, viewpoints, and principles that guide your life. Now contrast the sensations experienced yesterday with your present state. Note the difference.

• Exercise purposeful action. • Conduct oneself with deliberate intent. • Act with mindful deliberation. • Demonstrate conscious choice. Prior to rising from your sleeping quarters in the morning, establish your aspirations for the day. These represent distinct, precise objectives that you seek to establish or bring into fruition within your life on this particular day. Write these things down. Now, rise and set out to achieve your objectives. Be sure to bear them in constant consideration throughout the day to ensure their completion is not overlooked.

• Identify and acknowledge the elements for which you are grateful today, and convey your gratitude for them. The expression of gratitude possesses the inherent ability to profoundly transform one's life.

• The more you concentrate on something, the more it tends to expand, and what you devote your attention to has a tendency to materialize in actuality. Direct your attention solely towards the positive aspects and refrain from dwelling on anything negative. Irrespective of any circumstances that may arise today, adhere to this process and you shall enhance your self-esteem.

4. Embrace a more joyful demeanor by increasing the frequency of your smiles and laughter.

Expressing amusement and displaying a joyful countenance serve as direct antitheses to experiencing unpleasant emotions or negativity. Simply by incorporating this newfound practice into your daily routine, you will invariably experience a sense of well-being and optimism.

The body and mind exhibit a profound interconnection. Our thoughts and feelings are influenced by the manner in which we utilize our physical bodies.

A smile, even one that is contrived, has the capacity to induce an immediate heightened sense of happiness within oneself. This is a great way to lift your mood and spread positivity to those around you.

Try this exercise. Position yourself in front of a reflective surface, gaze at your reflection, and deliberately create a smile or emit a burst of laughter.

One can conjure a smile artificially, or one can contemplate a person, child, pet, situation, or any entity that brings about a smile. Both options will be highly effective.

It instantaneously imbues you with a sense of positivity." "It promptly instills within you a gratifying sense of positivity." "It swiftly engenders in you an overwhelming wave of positive emotions. Continue with your efforts, and you will find it impossible to refrain from wearing a smile on your face.

I strongly encourage you to immediately attempt it at this moment.

During the process of performing this exercise, I invariably find myself erupting into laughter. I also experience a strong sense of optimism... You have the capability to achieve similar results!

According to scientific research, laughter and smiling have been found to possess curative abilities against diseases and depression.

Frequently exhibit expressions of joy and amusement. It will enhance the overall positive atmosphere of your day and radiate outwardly to those in your vicinity. It is a mutually beneficial situation for all parties involved.

5. Exercise

A sound physical well-being is essential in maintaining an optimal state of mental wellness.

Physical activity not only alters your physical appearance, but it also has a transformative impact on your emotional state.

Engaging in physical activity enhances circulation throughout the entirety of the body, which encompasses the brain as well. It triggers an augmentation in the provision of oxygen and nutrients, which function as vital sustenance for the brain. In addition, a myriad of hormones are released, exerting influence on the enhancement of cognitive functions within the brain. The following hormones are included among them:

Endorphins: They mitigate stress levels and promote relaxation. Consequently, they aid in combatting anxiety and depression. Additionally, they alleviate pain and discomfort while promoting pleasure and elevating self-esteem.

Serotonin governs the regulation of appetite, enhances the quality of sleep, and influences emotional states. These elements are interconnected to facilitate a sense of happiness, relaxation, and positivity.

Dopamine serves as a neural transmitter that communicates signals of gratification and pleasure to the various centers within our brain. It governs our levels of motivation, thus influencing our degree of action in pursuit of our objectives.

Testosterone plays a crucial role in the physiological functioning of individuals regardless of their gender. It controls and oversees metabolic processes, muscle development, and sexual functioning. Insufficient testosterone levels can contribute to the development of depression and obesity.

The intended message is that if an individual remains inactive on their sofa for prolonged periods, they hinder the optimal functioning of their brain.

I strongly suggest allocating a minimum of 30 minutes each day to engage in physical activities such as walking, jogging, cycling, weightlifting, cardio exercises, yoga, or tai-chi of your choice. It is advisable to consult with your physician prior to commencing.

Furthermore, aside from the aforementioned morning exercise, it is recommendable to rise from your seat every half hour to engage in leg-stretching activities. Please engage in a brief stroll within the premises of the office. Please proceed to the water cooler, have a drink, and return. Kindly stand up and engage in some physical activity.

Please attempt to engage in both of these activities for a duration of 10 days. You will observe a significant enhancement in your levels of positivity and vitality. Engaging in physical activity rejuvenates the mind and body, infusing vitality into one's daily experiences.

6. Meditation

Our cognitive faculties are engaged in incessant contemplation throughout the day. It is inherently impossible to fully cease cognitive processes. Despite one's deliberate attempt to eradicate all thoughts, it will prove futile. In accordance with the tenets of Buddhist tradition, this phenomenon is commonly referred to as "the restless mind." Our thoughts and focus fluctuate in a highly erratic manner.

In order to achieve tranquility and contentment, it is imperative that we exert mastery over our own mental faculties. The pinnacle of liberty is found in the release from mental processes.

Imagine you are endeavoring to engage in a joyful and unrestrained exchange with your partner within the confines of your domicile, while your thoughts are preoccupied with the impending task of finalizing the project report before noon on the following day. What would be the level of effectiveness of that conversation?

The practice of meditation cultivates mindfulness, enabling individuals to reside in the current moment, thereby fostering an enhanced sense of well-being and resilience in the face of adversity. It has been demonstrated through extensive research that meditation serves as a highly efficacious therapeutic intervention for a range of prevalent ailments, while concurrently enhancing individuals' levels of happiness, empathy, and compassion towards their fellow beings.

Individuals who engage in the practice of meditation also report decreased levels of anxiety, anger, and mental stress, while concurrently noting an elevation in mindfulness, optimism, and tranquility. Meditation can serve as a beneficial technique for individuals who have undergone traumatic experiences.

The meditation technique that requires minimal effort: "

Please configure an alarm for a duration of 10–15 minutes.

Assume a comfortable seated position, ensuring your back remains relaxed and in an upright posture.

Kindly direct your attention towards your breath, and close your eyes to facilitate this inward focus. Take note of every aspect regarding it - from the moment it enters your olfactory system until it reaches your diaphragm. The cyclical ascension and descent of your abdominal region, and so forth.

In due course, your cognitive faculties will commence deliberating upon a subject. You will become engrossed in contemplation. One's attention dissipates from the breath and becomes fixated upon the thought at hand. It is perfectly acceptable. On those occasions when you find yourself giving undue attention to your thoughts rather than maintaining mindfulness of your breath, adopt a gentle and composed approach to redirect your focus back to your breath.

It is highly probable that you will once again lose your concentration and become immersed in contemplation. Once more, redirect your attention towards your breathing in a composed manner.

Continue performing this action until the sounding of your alarm.

This straightforward practice will significantly enhance the overall state of your mental faculties (such as tranquility, optimism, lucidity of thinking, attentiveness, determination, and single-mindedness). Its efficacy has been substantiated through extensive research conducted worldwide.

Try it yourself.

Enhance Your Proficiency in Resolving Conflicts

We all desire to effectively handle a situation with favorable results, or at the very least, mitigate any potential detrimental consequences. However, only a fraction of individuals possess the capability to accomplish such a feat. How frequently have you interceded in a situation and reached a mutually agreeable resolution?

Conflicts evoke heightened emotions within us, and if not appropriately addressed, can engender feelings of distress and letdown, potentially resulting in the deterioration of interpersonal connections.

Conflicts frequently serve as an indicator of robust relationships. When an individual is able to express their perspective to another individual, even in the presence of disagreement, it signifies an atmosphere of openness within the relationship, wherein both parties maintain an open line of communication. Nevertheless, it is during instances of discord that a multitude of adverse sentiments emerge. During combat, individuals may experience heightened levels of stress, anger, and fear. Due to the intense emotional state, there is a heightened likelihood of engaging in irrational behavior that can potentially harm the relationship. What measures do you employ to effectively handle this intricate predicament? How can both parties navigate this situation while preserving the fundamental integrity of the relationship, without resorting to deceit for the sake of politeness?

Consequently, what strategies can be employed to enhance one's conflict resolution aptitude?

Comprehend the discord

Amidst the conflict, it transcends mere discord. In a confrontational situation, the human body is compelled to maintain a heightened state of readiness, even in the absence of any actual danger. In order to comprehend the conflict at hand, it is crucial to recognize that, like oneself, the other individual is gripped by fear, leading to the realization that their concerns are not directed towards you.

Therefore, it is imperative to allocate sufficient time to comprehend the underlying factors that contributed to the emergence of the conflict. Were you in the wrong? If that is the case, it would be appropriate to offer a genuine apology. In the event that your partner was mistaken, it is possible to guide them towards recognizing their error in a considerate and non-patronizing manner.

In the course of this procedure, it is imperative to bear in mind that your contention lies not with the other individual, but instead, with a matter. Therefore, refrain from making comments pertaining to the individual and instead, consistently focus on the topic at hand. Instead of stating, "You are always hurting me," it is more appropriate to express, "Whatever you say always has a hurtful impact on me." By rephrasing this way, the emphasis is primarily on the impact of the person's words, rather than making a general accusation against them.

Comprehend the requirements of the other individual.

An additional aspect of conflict resolution entails consistently considering the perspective of the other party involved. With each exchange, endeavor to comprehend their perspective. Each individual is entitled to be treated with respect and have their viewpoints duly acknowledged. Hence, in order to enhance conflict management, it is vital to consistently bear in mind the inherent humanity of the other individual. It is our responsibility as human beings to comprehend and recognize the thoughts, emotions, necessities, and perspectives of others. In order to gain insight into their perspective and comprehend the reasoning behind their worldview, even if our own views may diverge from theirs.

Display a willingness to make concessions

We all experience the inclination to assert our correctness in a discordant situation. Hence, when the interlocutor expresses their viewpoint, you respond with your own opinion, leading to a situation where both parties engage in a heated debate without truly listening to one another. This exchange of emotions frequently culminates in the development of resentment and contributes to the continued deterioration of effective communication.

In order to enhance conflict management, it is imperative that active listening is employed by both parties involved, thereby facilitating a reciprocal exchange of ideas, ultimately culminating in a mutually agreeable compromise that duly acknowledges the perspectives of all individuals involved.

Engaging in compromise does not entail compromising on one's principles. On the contrary, it demonstrates your appreciation for the relationship and attentiveness towards the other person's needs.

Nevertheless, it is important to acknowledge the situations wherein you assume the sole responsibility of compromising, or when you are primarily responsible for making substantial concessions following a conflict. This unbalanced concession serves as an indication of an unhealthy relationship dynamic. Although it presents a formidable task to equitably divide settlement between both parties, the situation can be ameliorated by ensuring that neither party consistently bears the burden in every conflict.

Prioritizing the need to win an argument or be proven right consequently hinders one's willingness to attentively listen to the perspectives of others, thereby exacerbating the breakdown of communication.

Direct your attention to the conflict at hand.

In many instances, there is a prevailing temptation to incorporate past interactions into a fresh conflict. You and the other individual are engaged in a heated debate regarding the merits of purchasing a new item, when unexpectedly, you receive a favorable turn of events. Recall that occasion when you neglected to (insert unrelated matter here), you assert. Abruptly, it descends into an extended discourse between both parties focused on an unrelated matter that was not originally part of the day's dispute.

By clinging to the remnants of the past, our capacity to make reasoned judgments diminishes. Instead of seeking a resolution to the current discord, we embark on an investigative journey into the annals of history, aiming to unearth information that can substantiate your case or silence your interlocutor.

Exhibit a Readiness to Release

Releasing can be an exceedingly intricate endeavor, as one is frequently torn between the notion of truly relinquishing the matter at hand, or merely concealing it from view.

However, it is crucial to emphasize that it is imperative to address the matter prior to contemplating its abandonment. It is advisable for you to reach a point where you can assertively respond "no" when you contemplate whether the issue still perturbs you.

By choosing to conceal matters instead of addressing them directly, one may frequently experience persistent unease and merely defer their resolution. Therefore, it is advisable to make the decision to relinquish when you are in a state of reduced anger, stress, and volatility. This will enable you to carefully consider the consequences of your decision in a reasoned manner. If you continue to experience difficulty in relinquishing, it is possible that the matter has not yet been adequately resolved.

Choose Your Conflicts

It is not necessary for your input to be solicited in every potential conflict that arises. As you deepen your emotional awareness, you will gain the discernment to determine which endeavors merit your exerted diligence and which do not.

Conflicts are highly demanding circumstances and will deplete your energy reserves. It is crucial, therefore, to solely participate in conflicts that engender a discernible enhancement of one's perspective, overall well-being, and deeper comprehension.

Relationship/Social Awareness

How can one ascertain the true intentions of an individual who chooses not to be forthcoming in their communication? How might one effectively gain insights into an individual who resists disclosing their thoughts and emotions?

To cultivate emotional intelligence and derive personal growth from challenging experiences, it is imperative to extend one's comprehension of their own emotional state towards understanding the emotional being of others.

Developing and sustaining interpersonal connections is contingent upon one's possession of social consciousness.

By prioritizing the comprehension of the other individual beyond surface-level communication, one can enhance their overall understanding of said individual. Therefore, what are the methods employed to cultivate social awareness?

Number 9: The art of receiving and giving compliments

Accept compliments gracefully. Do not entertain suspicions of underlying intentions when receiving compliments. When receiving a compliment, it is advised that you refrain from displaying a dismissive response, such as rolling your eyes and uttering "Yeah, right" or shrugging it off. Please ensure that you express gratitude for the compliment by offering a smile and expressing thanks. Such a response will positively impact both the individual giving the compliment and yourself, the recipient, by fostering a sense of well-being and bolstering self-confidence. How to appropriately give compliments:

Exhibit genuine honesty by offering a compliment only when it is truly merited.

Please provide a concise and succinct response.

Please refrain from using any negative implications, such as expressing surprise at the quality of your presentation.

Refrain from engaging in self-deprecating comments when offering compliments, such as, 'You look incredibly stunning in that gown, I am certain I cannot compare.'

#10 Handling Criticisms

The adverse remarks from individuals can prove detrimental to your self-assurance, as they appear to insinuate a lack of worthiness or capability on your part. Do not permit oneself to experience harm or humiliation due to the critique. Place the criticism in proper context; prior to responding, ascertain the rationale behind someone's critique and its validity. If the circumstance is deemed unjust, steadfastly decline it. In the event that it is just or precise, kindly proceed with the following actions:

I concur with the critique without offering apologies or elaborations: 'You are correct, I indeed engaged in said action.' Thanks for telling me". This will effectively mitigate any disputes.

Inquire thoughtfully to ascertain the specific grievances of the critic. This will facilitate the transformation of criticism into a constructive dialogue.

#11 Take a risk

Explore novel, unfamiliar, and distinct experiences. Step outside your comfort zone. Engaging in unconventional behavior elicits a sense of self-satisfaction. In the event of your accomplishment, particularly in unforeseen circumstances, you can expect a significant surge in your self-assurance. Exert yourself and demonstrate your capabilities; cease evading fresh obstacles and retreating from uncomfortable circumstances or challenging individuals. It is important to bear in mind that self-assurance is akin to a muscle that can solely be strengthened through consistent and diligent exercise. While it is advisable to conduct a thorough examination of your apprehensions, refrain from excessively fixating on them. On the contrary, embrace the mantra: Confront the fear and proceed regardless!

#12 Maintain a well-groomed and presentable appearance

- Dress in appropriate attire - while it is true that clothing does not define an individual, one's appearance significantly impacts their posture, interpersonal interactions, and the way others respond to them.

- Maintaining personal appearance and hygiene – consistently ensure that one's appearance is professional, well-groomed, clean-shaven, and with neat hair.

- Maintain proper posture by aligning your spine, keeping your shoulders squared, lifting your head, and establishing eye contact, thereby exuding confidence and making a favorable impact on those around you.

- Physical fitness - Maintain a healthy lifestyle by engaging in regular physical activity to improve overall well-being both mentally and physically.

#13 Forgive and forget

Do you hold others accountable for your personal circumstances or the outcomes of your life? It is imperative to relinquish the victim mindset and embrace forgiveness. Compile a comprehensive inventory of individuals who have caused you distress, encompassing potentially diverse sources such as parental figures, educators, and former romantic partners. Make the commitment to sincerely grant forgiveness to each individual.

Please bear in mind that granting forgiveness does not equate to endorsing or endorsing the actions that transpired, but rather signifies your willingness to accept and reconcile with the past events. The deservingness of forgiveness by the perpetrators is immaterial; the crucial point is that you are engaging in forgiveness for your own sake, rather than theirs. You are relinquishing past grievances, acrimony, and animosity that have weighed you down and muddled your existence. You are making way for a plethora of new and fulfilling experiences. You are becoming free.

In conclusion, it is imperative that you remember to absolve yourself of any past shortcomings, refrain from excessive self-criticism, advocate for your own well-being, and acknowledge any harm you may have inflicted upon others.

#14 Focus on your strengths

Direct your attention towards your abilities, talents, and untapped potential rather than fixating on your shortcomings or limitations. Positive assertions have the potential to promptly elevate one's self-assurance. Comprehensively enumerate the aspects that you find favorable about your own character and proficient in, subsequently examining each item to identify opportunities for enhancing their utilization, identifying contexts where they can be more frequently employed, and exploring ways to amplify your capabilities. Identify virtues and competencies that you greatly appreciate and aspire to embody, such as resilience, empathy, meeting deadlines punctually, offering guidance to troubled youth, and more. For each attribute you have enumerated, ascertain the requisite steps to acquire it and diligently endeavor to attain it.

With every enhancement and achievement, your sense of self-assurance will ascend to a greater degree.

#15 Allocate additional time to associate with individuals who exemplify a positive, supportive demeanor.

Choose to be in the company of individuals who uplift and encourage you, rather than engaging with those who undermine and disparage you. What types of familial relations, social connections, or acquaintances do you possess? Can they serve as an exemplar in your endeavor to cultivate greater self-assurance? Do they possess attributes such as happiness, self-assurance, motivation, kindness, and optimism? If so, keep them. If not, it is advisable to minimize the amount of time spent with them or, if feasible, entirely refrain from their company due to the high likelihood of them impeding your progress. You and they are no longer birds of the same plumage.

Select literature or visual media that aligns with your pursuit of cultivating a greater sense of self-assurance. For instance, I possess a fondness for indulging in romantic novels; however, I am particularly discerning when it comes to avoiding literary works in which the main female protagonist is depicted as feeble, necessitating salvation, and significantly inferior to the male protagonist. The energetic, resilient, and intelligent female protagonist deeply connects with my sensibilities.

#16 Practice kindness and compassion towards others

Be kinder and helpful. There is an inherent sense of moral elevation in conscientiously extending assistance to individuals, particularly those who are unfamiliar to us. Have you had the pleasure of encountering such an elevation of the soul? It is not necessary for these actions to be prominently featured, but they can consist of commonplace gestures such as sincerely complimenting others, expressing gratitude, refraining from ridiculing others, and so on. When one decides to actively contribute to the betterment of other individuals' lives, they gain the realization that they hold the power to generate positive impact within the global community. This greatly enhances your level of self-assurance.

"#17 Addressing and correcting erroneous or pessimistic thought patterns

The perspectives one maintains regarding something may not be the sole conceivable way to perceive it. Additionally, these assertions may lack accuracy. Examine these thoughts in light of facts and logical reasoning to ascertain their accuracy, subsequently discarding any elements that prove to be incorrect or lacking factual basis.

These could potentially be subjective perceptions or viewpoints that have been impeding your progress. Especially, strive to refrain from:

Erroneously attributing emotions to reality- for instance, "I failed to observe a stair and consequently stumbled, thus displaying clumsiness.

Engaging in detrimental self-communication - For example, having the perception that I am dependable for creating chaos.

Forming unwarranted negative assumptions based on minimal or insufficient evidence, such as 'My friend did not extend an invitation to me for her party; she appears to perceive me as uninteresting.'

Transforming positives into negatives can be observed when one dismisses personal accomplishments, deeming them insignificant, such as stating "I only obtained this promotion due to the company's expansion".

What Factors Contribute To The Erosion Of Our Self-Confidence?

Considering the paramount importance of self-confidence, why do numerous individuals encounter difficulties in its cultivation? This inquiry implies that there existed a specific juncture in your existence during which you possessed an ample supply of self-assurance. Do you remember when? If you are unable to do so, please consider the remarkable courage exhibited by young children. Consider the resilience exhibited by young children as they persist in their efforts to stand upright, even in the face of discomfort resulting from previous stumbles. They move with an uncertain gait across the space, only to once again falter and aggravate the recently mended injuries on their knees. In their slightly more advanced years, they engage in the recitation of poems within bustling school auditoriums, occasionally faltering in their lines, yet persistently recommencing until reaching a resounding applause. Furthermore, they eagerly volunteer their viewpoints in response to inquiries posed within the classroom, exuding an unwavering sense of assurance in expressing their thoughts and emotions.

Observe the aforementioned individual, now in their adolescent years: it proves to be quite challenging to elicit a greeting from them towards visitors. Only those who possess complete certainty in their response and have the desire to engage in conversation will voluntarily raise their hands. Moreover, they have a tendency to refrain from delivering any form of public speech, regardless of the magnitude of the audience.

Now observe the mature individual who expresses a preference for enduring hunger over venturing into an unfamiliar dining establishment, or consistently selects a position towards the rear of the classroom, the place of worship, the gathering, and so forth.

Thus, may I inquire about the events that transpired during the intervening period? In addition to the apprehension arising from natural limitations and inherent consciousness of oneself and others, certain individuals experience a decline in their intrinsic assurance as a result of deficiencies in their upbringing and social interactions. These deficiencies consist of persistent condemnation, leading one to perceive oneself as lacking competency, resilience, or intelligence. Insufficient support from individuals of importance can consequently lead to the perception that your endeavors or accomplishments hold minimal value or that you do not hold significance in their eyes.

When individuals are subjected to comparison with others, even if the motive behind it is misguidedly to encourage personal growth, it inevitably erodes one's self-assurance. When my areas of weakness are brought to attention in comparison to your strengths, it leads to the depreciation of my abilities, talents, value, and undermines my self-assurance.

And we have previously discussed the presence of unattainable standards set by your parents and societal norms.

These examples represent merely a small selection of common instances that have the potential to continuously undermine one's self-assurance. The positive aspect, nonetheless, is that you have the ability to regain the self-assurance you once lacked and maintain it perpetually. Could you kindly explain the process? Acquire that knowledge in the following sections.

20 Highly Efficient Approaches to Enhancing Self-Confidence and Elevating Self-Esteem

Consider confidence to be akin to a muscle, similar to various muscles present in your physique. In order for muscles to operate efficiently, they ought to be in a state of optimal health, which can be achieved through the consumption of nourishing sustenance, ingestion of uncontaminated fluids, and consistent engagement in physical activity. This endeavor necessitates a significant investment of both your time and effort, whereas attaining the pinnacle of athletic performance necessitates substantially greater dedication and exertion.

This principle can similarly be attributed to the development of confidence within oneself. It exhibits growth in direct correspondence to the degree of performance demand placed upon it. The greater your efforts to utilize it, the greater its growth and the more effectively it serves you. Acquiring self-assurance thus becomes a progressive endeavor, necessitating meticulous attention and unwavering resolve, taken in small increments. It can be achieved by adopting the strategies delineated herein.

#1 Develop Self-awareness

Know yourself. What skills do you possess and what areas do you struggle in? In what aspects do you take pride in regarding your personal characteristics? Which aspects of your persona do you aspire to modify? What factors have impeded your ability to experience confidence?

"When responding to these inquiries, please contemplate your personal sentiments or opinions regarding your:

Physiognomic qualities - external presentation, level of physical wellness

Emotional disposition - do you typically exhibit a demeanor characterized by happiness, affection, serenity, and stability? Enumerate a comprehensive spectrum of emotions and evaluate your own disposition.

*Intellect –skills, qualifications

*Interpersonal skills – ability to navigate social situations with ease, perception of how others perceive you.

*Other attributes

Please provide candid feedback in order to avoid undermining the integrity of this needs/ability assessment exercise.

Once you have identified the gaps, determine the desired level of confidence at which you intend to function going forward. For instance, consider the situation wherein you experience apprehension towards conducting boardroom presentations; the desired level of confidence should be such that you are able to deliver presentations effortlessly while captivating your audience.

#2 Take Responsibility

Without fully acknowledging and embracing the indisputable fact that you alone bear the complete responsibility for the desired transformation in your self-assurance, and without demonstrating unwavering dedication to its attainment, you will be unable to make any substantive progress. You alone have the ability to cultivate your confidence. It is incumbent upon you to establish objectives, craft a strategic plan, and initiate decisive measures.

Henceforth, consider all occurrences as a result of your own actions. Henceforth, refrain from holding others accountable for:

* Your deficiency in or diminished self-assurance

The manner in which individuals interact with you

Your thoughts, expressions, or behaviors

Your instances of failure, adversity, and denial

Is there anything else pertinent to your personal history, aspirations, or present circumstances?

Assuming control will instill in you a sense of being akin to a unit manager, with the duty to fulfill production objectives, thereby nourishing a robust self-assurance.

#3 The way a person thinks determines their being.

Our thoughts shape our essence. Although this statement may appear trite, it is unquestionably factual. Your thoughts possess a profound capacity to shape the fabric of your reality. What are your thoughts regarding your own self-perception, abilities, and physical appearance? Do you tend to engage in pessimistic thinking? Do you frequently engage in thoughts such as:

I regret to inform you that I am unable to undertake this project at the moment.

Pursuing the opportunity to audition would yield minimal returns or I may not possess the necessary qualifications.

It is highly improbable that he harbors any genuine attraction towards me.

This pattern of pessimistic self-expression and negative thoughts serve to undermine your self-assurance and impede the full utilization of your innate abilities. Nonetheless, you possess the deliberate ability to select your thoughts and cognitive processes. In the present day, make the deliberate decision to adopt the mindset of an individual with unwavering self-assurance. Consequently, you shall experience an innate boost in confidence and exhibit a notable display of assuredness in your actions. "Under no circumstances, whether in thought or in verbal expression, should you:

*Put yourself down

*Say you can't

"*Declare that your desired outcome is unattainable "*Express the notion that achieving your objective is implausible "*Affirm that what you aspire for is beyond the realm of possibility "*State that the realization of your preferences is not feasible

*Adopt the belief that you possess no capacity to acquire fresh knowledge.

I strongly advocate for the cultivation of self-affirming thoughts and engaging in preparatory conversations with oneself.

By declaring statements such as "I possess the necessary qualifications to obtain that promotion," "I excel at..." and "I am determined to...," you actively reinforce positive beliefs and aspirations."

Engage in the habit of affirming positively! Individuals lacking confidence tend to exhibit an automatic tendency of declining or expressing uncertainty with a hesitant "no" or a vague "perhaps." Affirmative responses are indeed a reliable means to enhance one's self-assurance. It provides you with the motivation to undertake actions that you may not have previously been inclined towards.

#4 quieting the inner critic

Each one of us possesses an internal voice that tends to be negative in nature, relentlessly assaulting, evaluating, and censuring our actions - commonly referred to as the pathological critic. The critic expresses dissatisfaction and censure, holds you accountable when things go awry, draws comparisons between you and others, and highlights areas in which you fall short. It incessantly reminds you of your flaws, establishes unattainable benchmarks, and ruthlessly berates you for even the slightest errors. If left unaddressed, it has the potential to erode your self-assurance and undermine your sense of self-worth. May I inquire about your occupation? Engage in a dialogue with your critic, rendering their voice silent. However, the question remains: how does one accomplish this?

*Disrupt the derogatory thoughts with a resolute and assertive response, firmly dismissing them. Cease these disparaging criticisms immediately.

Assess the price of heeding the influence of one's inner voice on the advancement of one's professional path, interpersonal connections, and overall self-assurance. Are you willing to meet the financial obligation associated with this price? Not solely on this occasion, but conceivably on multiple occasions henceforth? Discard the negative thought and swiftly substitute it with a positive thought regarding your personal qualities, accomplishments, and the like.

Develop the habit of quieting the internal critic, and over time, you will undoubtedly witness an expansion of the collection of qualities that portray you as a person of confidence and capability.

#5 Avoid Perfectionism

Allow me to present to you one of my preferred adages - "Perpetual refinement is an eternal virtue, for it occupies the most expansive space within the abode." This indicates that achieving perfection is a considerable distance away, and it is unlikely that one will attain it. Hence, should you harbor the belief that every task must be executed flawlessly, genuine contentment with oneself or one's circumstances will ultimately elude you.

The pursuit of perfection may hinder one's ability to take action due to the fear of falling short of a prescribed standard. Consequently, you engage in procrastination, experience a shortage of time, fail to attain desired outcomes, and witness a decline in your self-esteem. Consequently, how do you address that issue?

"Strive for excellence; allocate the necessary dedication, time, and resources

Take pride in a task accomplished with excellence – refrain from dwelling on regretful 'what if' scenarios. Strive to achieve excellence with the resources at your disposal.

#6 Stop comparing

To commence, it is imperative to recognize that there will perpetually exist individuals in this world who surpass one's own capabilities in areas such as aptitude, aesthetic appeal, eloquence, intellect, charisma, and so on.

When engaging in comparisons, you are bound to consistently find yourself at a disadvantage. Therefore, it is advisable to aspire to become the best possible version of yourself, rather than settling for being a mediocre replica of someone else. So, what methods or strategies can be employed to accomplish this?

Direct your comparisons solely towards your own progress.

Reflect upon your accomplishments with a sense of pride and satisfaction, recognizing how far you have come.

Direct your attention towards self-improvement and refrain from making comparisons with others.

#7 Request what you desire

Cease hesitating or compromising for mediocrity. Why do you consistently engage in enduring silently? Indeed, your lack of confidence is becoming evident once more.

If you experience discomfort when it comes to expressing your desires or voicing dissatisfaction with unsatisfactory service, it is likely that you harbor apprehensions of causing offense, appearing discourteous, or encountering rejection. However, as a direct consequence, one's self-perception of worthiness or value diminishes, leading to a tendency to attribute mistreatment to others. In addition, you allowed the opportunity to rectify or enhance the situation to elapse.

On the contrary, individuals who exude confidence exhibit assertiveness in requesting their desired outcomes, proactively determine their rightful entitlements, and adamantly decline anything less than what they deserve. They prefer to accept the possibility of rejection over excessively contemplating an abundance of thoughts filled with speculative statements such as 'perhaps I should have...' and 'what if I had...?' How does one navigate such a situation?

"Ensure there is a clear and definitive understanding of your desired outcome in your thoughts.

Do not engage in unnecessary circumlocution. Start with 'I want..'

Refrain from employing apologetic language, such as phrases like 'I am afraid...' or 'I am sorry but...' These expressions may create an impression of uncertainty, potentially leading to being disregarded.

In some instances, consider offering a suggestion rather than asserting a direct demand, such as by posing the question, 'Would it not be more advantageous if you...?'

If your request is declined, remain resolute and politely reiterate it until it receives due consideration. Do not hesitate to express your desires, even if it leads to being perceived as persistent.

4.4 Connection

A significant portion of our population maintains excessively solitary existences. There exists an inherent and commendable inclination in human nature to seek communal connection, and it would be remiss to deprive oneself of this pursuit. Presently, one may possess a romantic relationship, companions, and kinship. However, a considerable number of individuals fail to meet the criteria for inclusion in one or more of these categories. Allow us to discuss each individual.

The initial, an amorous connection, frequently serves as a catalyst for anxiety and dissatisfaction amongst a considerable number of individuals. Numerous individuals experience a sense of isolation and perceive a lack of reciprocated romantic interest in their lives. They may isolate themselves from society. Another scenario arises when individuals become socially ostracized due to prevailing biases and societal expectations imposed on them by the world at large. Many individuals encounter difficulties due to an excessive number of relationships in their lives. They possess adeptness in socializing and locating individuals, however, they lack proficiency in managing interpersonal connections. They will engage in a detrimental interpersonal connection and perform actions solely to maintain the continuity of the relationship.

These individuals are frequently referred to as codependent. Codependent individuals often perpetuate the suffering of others due to their own existing state of distress. They desire to uphold the status quo and maintain a sense of authority, while also demonstrating aversion to exposing their vulnerabilities. Frequently, individuals who exemplify codependency tendencies will consciously choose to remain in an unhealthy relationship due to an overwhelming fear of its termination. Frequently, individuals lacking a strong sense of self are prone to becoming overly engrossed in the lives of others and readily developing intimate connections. Individuals who display codependent tendencies often struggle with independent living and possess a stronger preference for being in an unhealthy relationship over having no relationship whatsoever.

Both categories of individuals, namely those who tend to avoid social interactions and those who display codependent characteristics, will be required to cultivate their ability to open up in order to establish fresh connections. Each individual faces distinct obstacles based on their personality traits, yet at its core, their fundamental objective should be to foster greater openness and establish deeper, more significant relationships.

The introverted individual, or the individual who typically exhibits a preference for solitude, will need to adopt an openness towards engaging in social activities and participating in enjoyable interactions with others. It is understandable that the introvert may initially experience a sense of unease or discomfort, yet with increased exposure to social occasions, one's level of comfort will inevitably escalate.

Presented here is an illustrative anecdote outlining a standard developmental timeline observed within this domain. This may not universally align with individuals' character, but it is a plausible outcome. Mark is a resident of Ontario. Mark experienced a rather conventional upbringing in a suburban locale, engaging in customary pursuits associated with a young boy from his community. However, he reached a juncture where he became cognizant of his inability to establish satisfactory connections with others. Mark's parents frequently engaged in conflicts with one another, and they exhibited a limited inclination towards nurturing interpersonal relationships. Frequently, they would display a sulking demeanor within the confines of the residence, engaging in disputes or exhibiting signs of temperament and aggression. Mark acquired the discernment to maintain distance from individuals and exercise caution when placing trust, as the concept of friendships did not align with the paradigm of life that his parents instilled in him. Friendships were considered as additional, presences that could be acquired if one had the luxury of time, but were generally treated as secondary matters.

Mark commenced his secondary education and associated himself with a group of individuals who possessed intellect but also exhibited a penchant for engaging in disruptive behavior. During lunchtime, they would covertly make their way to the restrooms in an attempt to evade their obligations for the remainder of the afternoon, emerging only upon the sound of the final dismissal bell. They occasionally provoked the ire of educators due to their mischievous nature and inclination towards creating disruptions. However, the educators eventually acknowledged that these individuals were highly intelligent and exceptionally bright youngsters, whose curiosity and thirst for new experiences were simply inherent aspects of their nature.

Mark ultimately completed his high school education and subsequently pursued higher studies at an esteemed art institution located in Rhode Island. He commenced his classes with a tinge of hopefulness and nervous anticipation, and before long, he found himself immersing deeply into the captivating realm of the art world. He commenced acquainting himself with fellow artists of his generation, thus finding his place within a community. The decisive moment in his process of becoming more outgoing occurred when he formally acquainted himself with a fellow art club member. It was the late afternoon of that day when Mark made his way towards his dormitory on foot.

While immersed in the melodies emanating from his headphones, he perceived the presence of an artfully arranged table positioned outside the edifice dedicated to creativity. He muses within his own mind, "I do not typically possess the inclination to approach and present myself," yet he proceeds to undertake the action, expressing to them, "Greetings, I am known as Mark." I have a profound passion for art, and I find great interest in the endeavors you are undertaking." Initially, his unassuming persona elicits laughter from them, yet they soon recognize the sincerity behind his words and begin acquainting themselves. They perceive Mark's artistic viewpoint to be quite commendable, and consequently, they express a desire to extend an invitation for his inclusion in the club. Mark's initial shyness dissipated as he ventured beyond his comfort zone and pursued an auxiliary interest, such as art, which enabled him to establish meaningful connections within his community.

The emergence of a friendship is indeed a profoundly exquisite phenomenon. Initially, one tends to form preconceived notions about an individual, taking into account factors such as their manner of speech, choice of attire, and age. Subsequently, as you interact with the individual, you observe a harmonious rapport between the two of you. Subsequently, you commence to allocate time in their company and discern that you thoroughly enjoy their company. Subsequently, a subtle shift in perspective occurs. One may perceive the disparities between their initial impressions of an individual and their true nature. This situation may give rise to some confusion, albeit ultimately being a natural phenomenon. Subsequently, a more profound connection is established with the individual, leading to the realization of a sense of trust in them. You place your trust in them due to the extensive experience you have had dealing with them, which has afforded you a comprehensive understanding of their character and behavior patterns.

To achieve this outcome, it is imperative for you to display a willingness to be receptive and forthcoming. Fundamentally, a pervasive apprehension is present within all interpersonal connections. The reliability of an individual's presence or absence is contingent upon the trust placed in them.

It is inherent for individuals to exhibit tendencies towards seclusion. Numerous individuals acquire such behavior/traits. Indeed, one could surmise that a substantial portion of individuals adopt such behavior as a means of safeguarding themselves. Individuals tend to adopt a closed-off demeanor as a means of evading their emotions, rather than actively engaging in the challenging and uncomfortable task of confronting them. A person resorts to isolating themselves when they are overwhelmed with their workload and are uncertain about how to proceed.

Existence does not constitute a festival of suffering. Undoubtedly, within it lie carnivals, among which some can be classified as carnivals of agony. One has the option to remunerate for participation in these carnivals, which can prove to be rather captivating in their distinctive manner. Nevertheless, individuals harboring an excessively pessimistic outlook on the world are inadvertently causing detriment to both themselves and those around them. All objects that ascend will inevitably descend. In accordance with Newton's Third Law, every action is met with an equal and opposing reaction. These principles constitute the fundamental principles of entropy. Entropy asserts that our existence within the cosmos is characterized by an inherent tendency towards decay and disintegration. It is a location that is predestined for insignificance, much like its state prior to its establishment. Entropy, in essence, dictates that if there exists a concentration of thermal energy in a particular area of the room, it will not persist in that location. It will undergo expansion and ultimately disperse. It is equivalent to the entirety of the universe. All things are gradually diminishing. Humans will progress far more rapidly than the Earth, as the Earth came into existence in the distant past and has consistently persevered since then. The essence of human existence does not primarily manifest in such a manner.

Indeed, human existence can be likened to a fleeting moment, akin to a brief cinematic sequence within the vast expanse of time, which resembles somber obscurity within the confines of a theater. It possesses such minuscule dimensions and such inconspicuous nature that comprehending it becomes arduous. In what manner do we achieve the capacity to experience instances of absolute uninhibited delight, euphoria, and genuine camaraderie? Why does anything matter?

It falls upon you to make this determination, as others cannot ascertain this answer on your behalf. It is imperative that you actively interact with the inquiry and independently determine the responses. Nevertheless, by observing your surroundings and maintaining a receptive mindset, it is certain that you will encounter joy in the world. It is highly improbable that you will be unable to find joy in your current circumstances. You will find something. There could potentially be an evening when you witness a sunset that leaves you in awe. It has the capacity to elicit an emotional response, possibly invoking tears. It is possible that this dinner could be exceptional. One must endeavor to discover avenues for experiencing delight in our existence as human beings. Every individual possesses the capability within themselves, and it is within the reach of all to discover it.

Are you familiar with the factors that facilitate this process? Allowing oneself to cultivate connections and engage in meaningful interactions, embracing the necessary facets of human experience through interpersonal relationships. This may encompass individuals who belong to one's family, acquaintances, romantic partners, or other types of interpersonal connections. Regardless of the circumstances, it is imperative that you strive to cultivate an inclination to embrace such relationships. Once you succeed in doing so, you will discover an unparalleled level of congruity with another individual. In order to establish true connection with another individual, it is imperative to wholeheartedly engage with them, immersing oneself in the present moment and conscientiously directing our attention towards it. One's thoughts may occasionally drift, leading to feelings of distraction or unease; however, it is always possible to refocus one's attention on the present moment, fostering presence and connection with oneself and the individual in question.

www.ingramcontent.com/pod-product-compliance
Lightning Source LLC
Chambersburg PA
CBHW050238120526
44590CB00016B/2136